TED Talk Secrets

Storytelling and Presentation Design for Delivering Great TED Style Talks

All rights Reserved. No part of this publication or the information in it may be quoted from or reproduced in any form by means such as printing, scanning, photocopying or otherwise without prior written permission of the copyright holder.

Disclaimer and Terms of Use: Effort has been made to ensure that the information in this book is accurate and complete, however, the author and the publisher do not warrant the accuracy of the information, text and graphics contained within the book due to the rapidly changing nature of science, research, known and unknown facts and internet. The Author and the publisher do not hold any responsibility for errors, omissions or contrary interpretation of the subject matter herein. This book is presented solely for motivational and informational purposes only.

Your Free Gift 1

Introduction.. 2

Chapter 1: Public Speaking Today.. 4

Chapter 2: The Idea 9

Chapter 3: Outlining And Writing Your Speech 15

Chapter 4: Improving Your Speech: Slides, Visual Aids And Transitions 26

Chapter 5: Practice Makes Perfect.................................... 37

Chapter 6: Own Your Talk 42

Conclusion 45

Additional Resources 47

Your Free Gift

As a thank you for reading *Ted Talk Secrets*, I would like to give you a copy of *The Most Popular TED Talks of All Time*. This gift is a perfect complement to this book and will help you along your journey. Visit http://www.deepthoughtpress.com/ted-talks to download your free gift.

Introduction

Thank you for reading "TED Talk Secrets: Storytelling and Presentation Design for Delivering Great TED Style Talks".

This book will provide you everything that you need to learn about how you can deliver a great TED style talk and capture your target audience.

TED Talk is one of the most popular forms of public speaking today, thanks to its stimulating way of delivering short lectures. With this book, you will learn how you can make your lectures become as life-changing as your favourite TED Talks and make sure that you hit your goals when delivering your ideas that are worth spreading.

With this book, you can discover how you can make sure that your idea is delivered using the best possible methods to make your lecture short and personal, and more importantly, deliver the maximum impact to your audience. At the same time, this book will see to it that you provide yourself the right elements to ensure the success of your speech, starting from generating the best ideas that would present you as a field expert, to using presentation tools that would best supplement your speech.

If you are ready to make that big concept in your head make a big impact, then this book is for you.

Chapter 1: Public Speaking Today

Think about the last time you heard someone give a speech or a presentation. What about the last time you attended a graduation and heard the commencement speaker talk? For sure, it can be pretty boring because

1. It was so long that your mind drifted off somewhere.

2. There was simply too much information being conveyed that you got lost.

3. The speaker was just talking all about himself and his achievements.

Whatever the reason was, it can sure be uninspiring. It didn't draw a reaction from you. You can see a good talk or speech if it fires up an audience, and this didn't.

Recent studies show that a person's memory works well if the data presented to him is given in a limited amount of time. Time has brought forth a lot of improvements in making a presentation or a speech. People have learned to use slides and visual aids in order to improve their points. And one of these modern talks is Technological, Entertainment, and Design, simply known as TED talks.

WHAT IS TED?

With the slogan "Ideas worth Spreading", TED was founded in 1984 to feature prominent personalities who give talks that range from five to eighteen minutes. Eventually, it spread over the globe, allowing independent organizations to hold their own set of talks, named as TEDx.

Soon enough, off-shoots like TEDWomen, TEDMed and country-based ones like TEDIndia came about. TED employed well-known individuals such as Bill Gates, Bill Clinton, Al Gore, Bono, Larry Page, Sergey Brin, and even Nobel Prize winners to give talks on different topics, ranging from the initial technological, entertainment and design topics to more globally-inclined and universal ones like climate change, terrorism, gender equality and more.

Needless to say, TED has set the standard for public speaking in modern times. Videos of TED presentations have gone viral and have been viewed up to a million times. It's not doubt that TED speakers have worked extremely hard to create presentations that will be popular on the Internet. Many online viewers of TED talks have expressed inspiration upon watching these awesome talks.

In this book, we will tackle how you can become an effective speaker and organize your own TED-style talk. No matter how great your idea is, it is your delivery that will determine if your message is received and understood by your desired audience. If you cannot communicate your thoughts persuasively in today's information age your ideas simply won't matter.

TED Talks Vs. Your Usual Speeches

TED talks differ from your usual business presentations in two main ways: their production and their approach. What production means is the delivery.

It would be observed that TED talks are delivered without notes and thus from the memory of the speaker. However, these talks are not given on an impromptu. Rather, they are carefully rehearsed scripts that often take months to create. In most business presentations, you would see presenters with notes while delivering their speeches. In TED talks, these notes are often in the presentation slides that the audience sees while the presenter is speaking.

One would also take on the production value of the TED talk. For example, if the speaker brings in a toy or a piece of paper, it would automatically play an important role in the talk. Most often, these props are brought to draw in audience impact. In most prestigious TED talks these visual aids are well-lit. In fact, TED talks organized by the official organization make use of a lot of camera angles in order to make the presentation have that 'cinematic' feel. The videos you would see on the official website of TED are all skilfully recorded and edited presentations by several well-known people in their chosen fields.

But the most introspective difference of TED-style talks amongst other speeches is the APPROACH. Here are the reasons why:

1. TED Talks Are Personal

Passion is the key reason why people give TED talks. When you feel passionate about a certain topic or field, it creates an energy boost that can be easily passed on to your audience.

2. TED Talks Allow You to Travel

The speaker allows you to take a journey by explaining the truth about what he is passionate about. He or she might be just someone speaking in front of you, but as you would then observe, the speaker moves from ignorance to knowledge by talking about his or her passion. It might start off with a simple question to the audience but as the speaker moves along, the question branches out to deeper ones, thus creating a complex yet meaningful process of how to get there, like business presentations do.

3. TED Talks Keep It Short and Simple

Usually, TED talks are limited to a maximum of 18 minutes – a reason why speakers will cut to the chase than most public speakers do. In business and public presentations, one would always observe people who are always beating around the bush, pushing in adjectives and other flowery contents. TED talks would cut off any irrelevant ideas and make everything count.

4. TED Talks have that "A-HA!" Moment

TED talks have that intensity that makes you shift around your seat. You would think that speeches are boring, but TED talks have a unique factor that engages the audience, making them feel important. You wouldn't think much of what is happening to our climate, but watching Al Gore's Inconvenient Truth would make you think that you have to be involved. TED talk has that kind of breakthrough moment that makes you feel that something big is at stake.

Chapter 2: The Idea

Selecting an idea for a talk can sometimes be a crisis. You get ideas from daydreaming. You get ideas from being bored. You get ideas all the time, but for a TED-style talk, that idea should be able to be warped into an engaging topic. That means that you need to generate a concept that is worth talking about. When you think about it, you need to generate that idea that would be worth remembering and spreading around.

Where Do Good Ideas Come From?

Steven Johnson, Steven Johnson in his TED Talk pondered about the emergence of coffee shops in England in 1650. He flashed a single picture of the Grand Cafe in Oxford to his audience, explaining that in the early

English days, alcohol was the beverage of choice, since drinking water was not safe.

You would have an entire English population drunk every day, people who cannot think clearly as they were intoxicated. Apparently, Grand Cafe was the first coffee shop in England, which was then followed by a number of coffee shops, resulting in a shift of choices of drinks that then transpired the great Enlightenment. People who sobered themselves up as they discover the stimulating effects of caffeine, people who started to think more clearly – providing innovation for the country, which was dubbed as the Enlightenment.

"But the other thing that makes the coffeehouse important," Steven Johnson continues, "is the architecture of the space." The birth of the coffee shop enabled other people with different expertise and historical backgrounds to share their ideas clearly. It is as if the coffee house is a conjugal bed for ideas to get together.

We all have these innate ideas and when we discover other people that have their own set of ideas, we learn from them. People get out from the coffee shop taking fragments of ideas that others had imparted and most likely had thought about them while having dinner.

And that is what great about ideas. It can be moulded together. It can be found innately or discovered by meeting people, encountering even a simple life experience.

Find The Jewel In Your Expertise, Passion And Experience

Eman Mohammed, the only female photojournalist based in Gaza Strip, Palestine. Three weeks into starting her career, the Gaza War broke out.

Eman spoke about the sexual harassment she received from her own colleagues and the dangers of working during war. While her words are short, she made it clear that her experiences in Gaza affected her and that she would like to for people to hear out her story.

TED Talks tap on people who are not necessarily expert on their field but has an adept knowledge on the ins and outs of their chosen topic. This has to be something that is close to your heart, so that you can freely express and go about the topic in front of your audience.

In choosing a main idea for your talk, you can tap on these three things:

1. Expertise

2. Passion or frustration

3. Experience

Looking back to our example above, Eman's talk can fall in any of the three. While she might not be the greatest photojournalist, her experience in being the sole one in Gaza Strip provides a compelling tale that she alone can share. It is her passion to be a photographer – a move that was shunned by the uptight culture in her home. With that, she has to struggle with the consequences of her passion, and lives to share her experiences in TED.

Your Idea Doesn't Have To Be Complicated

In 2012, Joe Smith spoke to a local audience at TEDxConcordiaUPortland about the proper use of a towel paper. "You use paper towels to dry your hands every day," he argues, "but chances are, you're doing it wrong."

Smith proceeded to show everybody that he can dry his wet hands by using just one piece of a paper towel.

The idea was so simple yet engaging because everybody uses paper towels. It is the simplicity that captivated the audience to listen to Smith, as well as the familiarity of the problem he imposed.

Picking an idea for a TED-style talk doesn't have to sound so ambitious. It could range from simple to controversial ones, but the key point is the delivery of the message.

You wouldn't pick a topic that you cannot defend, play with and express passionately, right?

Most importantly, this should be something that they can relate to. There were a lot of interactions that Joe Smith got from the audience because speaking about paper towels is easy. Everybody uses them.

It was easy to talk about something that everybody knows. The real deal here is to talk about something that they think they know.

Consult Your Idea

Once you have an idea in mind, you can write it down and consult your trusted peers about it. Moreover, refer to someone who is not an expert in your chosen topic.

Ask yourself these questions:

1. Is this new?

Are you prepared to tell people something that is fresh for them? Have you already researched about this idea and see if anyone has already talked about it? If yes, do you consider taking a new angle?

2. Is it interesting?

Do you think that your idea can be applied to someone's day-to-day life? Do you think that this is something that people will care about? Do you think that people will find this relevant?

3. Is it true?

Are you presenting a new research? Are you sure that this is backed up with data and is already reviewed? Are you presenting a realistic situation? Do you aim for your audience to do something about it?

If you find some difficulty in answering yes to these set of questions, you should review your idea. Confidence in your chosen topic will pave way to a great talk.

Chapter 3: Outlining and Writing Your Speech

After finding your main idea, your next move is to compose an outline for your talk. Structuring your upcoming speech would be easier if you break it down to simple, major details.

The most effective way of delivering a speech is to break it down to three major parts:

1. Introduction

2. Body

3. Conclusion

Some professionals include TRANSITION as part of the main components of the speech. It takes practice and little bit of expertise in order to safely shift from one topic to another. That is why speakers also practice the transitioning of their main ideas from one point to another.

The INTRODUCTION makes up approximately ten percent of a speech. Yet, it is the crucial part to form in order to draw in your audience members. These first words provide ultimately the foundation for all the information that follows, and gives a preview of all the main points that you wish to go through in your talk.

In the three-act structure of cinema, the first act is called the exposition. In this period, main characters and the main plot are introduced. Same way in public speaking, making an introduction is the way of exposing your audience to your idea. Now, first impressions last. A strong introduction is the make or break moment in which the audience would decide if they want to listen to you or not.

Introductions vary and it might include stories, quotations, a hypothetical question, a picture flashed in front of the audience and other visual aids. A good introduction provides a clear framework for your message, and it makes the audience want to hear what you have to say. Moreover, this is the part where you stake a claim, or give the entire statement of your speech.

Here are a few things you would want to keep in mind when making an introduction:

1. Some public speakers would often start writing or outlining their speeches by focusing on the main content first. Since the introduction is the part that paves the way for the main message, it would be helpful to write first the body. Knowing your main message will ensure that the introduction is complete and relevant to your main idea.

2. Your first words will be the deciding factor whether they will or will not listen to you. If your talk is designed to focus on something that your audience is very much aware of, start with a clear statement of what it is. If it is something new, try to have your audience relate to it by implying the new one to something that they are aware of. Try something funny by surprising your audience with some cool facts, but do not bore them with a lot of figures.

3. Identify the focus of your talk. Speeches all have a purpose: to inform, entertain, persuade, argue or even to make people act upon a certain issue. After getting the audience interested in the general purpose, let them know what narrow aspect of it you will focus on in your speech.

4. In your introduction, it would be helpful to give a preview on your main points. This gives your audience a guide for your message and helps them to follow along.

5. Make sure that your introduction is compelling. Don't go around thanking the organizers that you're glad to be there. Don't mention all of the VIPs in the room that would take up much time. Remember that TED-style talks run for 18 minutes max. You have 60 seconds to make a compelling introduction or the audience would

start using their cell phones to play games or to check email.

6. Keep in mind that all things predictable are boring. Try to surprise your audience by jumping right into the story, presenting an intriguing slide or counter-attack an insight that is relevant to modern times or current beliefs.

Once you have captured your audience by giving a smashing introduction, it is time to move to the real meat of your TED-style talk: the CONTENT or the BODY. The body should take up about 75% of your entire speech time, since this is where you will go into detail about your main points.

Establish Your Purpose

Now, after claiming your audience, it is time for them to realize the purpose of your speech. In your introduction, you have given people a sneak-peek of what your content would look like. Generally, a person gives speeches to entertain, inform or to argue about something. Each purpose has a slightly different approach in order to convey the objectives to the audience. Once purpose is established, you can now begin a strategy to achieve that same purpose with your main key points.

Determine Your Main Points

Main points are major ideas or arguments found in the body of your talk. These ideas (points) are provided to the audience in a preview that you have given in the introduction.

Once your purpose has been established, it's time to move on by exposing the main points of your talk.

Here are few tips in making the main points of your TED-style talk:

1. You'll want to start by brainstorming a list of all possible main points to support your purpose. Organize your thoughts in a cohesive, logical flow. You can do this with a set of friends or people that you trust.

2. Remember that your main points should support the purpose of your talk.

3. Avoid too many jargons, technical terminologies that would take time to explain.

4. Some points can be nested under main points. By ranking the points of your speeches based on their relativity and importance, you can create a hierarchy of details and sub-details.

5. Your main content should be creative and engaging. Do not lose the interest that you have gained by your introduction. Use a variety of examples to illustrate the main points of your speech, from research, facts and figures, to personal anecdotes and references.

6. Don't stray too far. Remember the framework of your message. Having too much stories would make you wander off the topic. Take off things that do not belong in your speech or are irrelevant to your subject.

7. Don't let citations interrupt the flow of your explanation. As much as possible, present more empirical data than anecdotes.

8. Be yourself. Do not be afraid to let your personality mould with your speech. Match it with your approach.

Keep it Short and Simple

Ultimately, you'll want to boil down your main points to no more than three or four points. This might seem to short or minimalistic, but remember that your audience will only be able to remember so much. An article in Fortune written by Anne Fisher says "With an attention span of five minutes, the average audience is going to tune out 84% of your 30-minute speech unless, that is, you find ways to keep them interested."

As TED talks run only at the maximum of 18-minutes, and let's say that you have a minute or less to give an introduction. You would need to consider breaking down your main points into few ones. The best messages are short and easy to understand as they are easy to remember.

Tell a Story

Every great speech has a story. Great speakers like Abraham Lincoln, Barack Obama, Bill Clinton, Steve Jobs, Neil Gaiman, and even Jesus Christ included stories to convey their message to their audiences. Stories always touch people, as well as giving examples in order to clear a point. And it could be observed that story-telling is one of the running themes in TED-style talks.

Nancy Duarte, a TEDxEast Interconnectivity speaker said that a way to effectively convey an idea is through story. She said that illiterate people managed to pass on lessons to generations on to the next generations and they would stay whole. So there's something exquisite in stories that makes it so when it was amassed, can be taken in and then remembered by recipient of the message.

A story can be a compelling evidence to support a main point in your talk. For some speeches, evidence can be in the form of statistics, data or historical facts. Depending on your topic, audience and venue, humour may also be appropriate for your talk.

Nancy Duarte tells the TEDx listeners in the conference that sometimes, our ideas are new and fascinating, but it can be rejected. Some recipients might favour an average idea because it was presented much sexier or nevertheless more appealing. And if you can communicate a message that resonates, change can happen. You can change the world.

Dive into a story. Show your passion.

Drawing the Conclusion

If the body of the speech is the main course, the conclusion or the ending is the icing on the cake. While the body makes up seventy five percent of your speech and the introduction is about ten percent, the conclusion should cover the rest of your message.

Like the introduction, you would have to write your conclusion last. The introduction and conclusion of your speech serve as header and footer to your speech's body, so it only makes sense that you'll want to jot them down after you have constructed your main points.

Going back to the three-act structure, the conclusion features the resolution of the story and its subplots. This is the time to answer the questions you have stated in the introduction and to give the point of realization in the story. Like also in public speaking, this is where you tie loose ends and the landing point where the audience would feel positive towards you and the idea you have presented.

Most of the time, the conclusion of your speech will be what people would mostly remember after leaving. This is as important as grabbing the listener's attention in the introduction. You need to leave them a lasting impression.

The purpose of the conclusion is to summarize your main points and to prepare the audience for the end of your speech. You'll want to recapture the essence of your speech: your main points and the purpose of why you spoke about it. It is especially important to remember that the conclusion of your speech is not the time to introduce new points or new supporting evidence; doing so will only confuse the audience. Conclusion is the final touch that makes your speech stand out.

Use Transitional Phrases

While your introduction can be something unpredictable and shocking to capture the audience's attention, you would have to avoid that in your ending. The last thing you want is for the audience to be caught off guard as you ended your speech. It would be helpful to use transitional words such as "finally", "in conclusion" or "in summary". The audience will caught on that you are about to end your talk and would pay attention to your final words.

Don't Try to Sell

Avoid promoting yourself to the audience. Remember that your speech is something that should inspire people to act upon something. Avoid using corporate logos, book covers and other products. Don't mention the upcoming novel you are writing, or the product that your company wants the audience to buy. TED talks are not done to in order to sell a speaker's products or services. But doing an excellent talk can help someone's visibility and feasibility to increase.

Recap your Main Points

This is your chance to restate what you have said earlier in the main body. While summarizing your main points is important, be wary of simply repeating your main points word for word. You have to paraphrase and reconstruct your main points rather than repeat what you said from the speech's body. This will allow you to capture the essence of your speech.

End on a High Note

Ask yourself these questions: What do I want the audience to remember after this speech? What do I want them to recollect after this? The conclusion is your take-home message. This should be memorable.

Some speakers opt to share a quotation or an anecdote. Nancy Duarte chose to spoke about her personal life at the end of her Tedx speech and concluded, "I could let all these things push me down, and I could let all these ideas die inside of me. You know that it's just too hard to change the world, life is just too tough. But I chose a different story for my life... It's not really the whole world that I could change, but you know that you could change your world, you can change your life, you can change the whole world that you have control of. You can change your sphere. I want to encourage you to do that, 'cause you know what? The future isn't a place that we go; it is a place that you get to create." And then she pointed to the audience, "I wanna thank you."

It's important to remain relatable and credible to the audience up until your final word, so be sure to craft your conclusion in a way that is still appropriate.

At the end of your speech, it is important to address how your idea could affect your audience if they were to accept it.

With all of these in mind, remember that one of the most important things that a TED-style talk can do is to call people to action. A great speech must be something that compels people to do something and inspire people to reflect on things around them.

There is no way for someone to determine the ultimate formula for a great speech. Audiences are unpredictable and the circumstances that you encounter while delivering one can often affect the outcome of your presentation.

However, starting with an attention-grabbing statement or technique, telling stories that everyone could somehow relate to, reiterating your main points and crafting a great memorable last line will give you a good foundation for your speech.

Also, one of the great ways to convey a message is to support it visually, with the use of props and presentation slides.

Chapter 4: Improving Your Speech: Slides, Visual Aids and Transitions

TED-style talks do not stray far from your usual presentations. Speakers also use pictures, slides, and videos to convey a message. Now, why would you use props or visual aids in your talk? If you have prepared your script well and you managed to focus on your main point, shouldn't it stand alone by itself?

Presentation slides has several functions: it can serve as a transition from one point to another, it can improve your audience's understanding of your message, it can add spice and interest to your speech, enhance not only your credibility but also the audience's ability to retain the message.

Why You Should Use Slides or Visual Aids

Dr. Jill Bolte Taylor, an American neuroanatomist, author, and public speaker at the February 2008 TED Conference talk held a human brain in front for everybody to see while speaking, "If you've ever seen a human brain, it's pretty clear that these two hemispheres are separate from one another."

"I have here a real human brain. So this is a real human brain."

Slides can be helpful for the audience, but they are by no means necessary or relevant to every talk. Ask yourself: Would my slides help and clarify information for the audience, or would they distract and confuse them?

Let us examine the functions of having visual aids in a presentation.

I. Transition

A quite number of people would be surprised to know that transitions are one of the four major keys of a speech. A transition is a change or shift from one topic to another. Actually, transitions are crucial for public speakers as they do not have headers and chapters that writers can create by formatting their written works. In a written speech, you can see chapters and breaks to indicate paragraphs and new messages.

Speakers can imitate these signs and signal transitions using visual aids and body language.

II. Slides Can Help Better Understanding

When you think about it, communication is really complex. Most of the time, simple things get misinterpreted because of the way you deliver them. Like in everyday conversations between individuals, misunderstandings are bound to happen in holding a talk.

Thing is, perception and interpretation are both high human processes. Think of it like those optical illusion images you see on the web. You can see a horse in the picture, or you can see that the drawing can be a frog instead. Or maybe you would see four lines, but when you look at it, it can be six, depending on how you look at the visuals. This would depend on the perception of the one looking at the photograph.

To reduce or avoid misunderstanding in your TED-style talk, presentation aids can be used to clarify or to emphasize. Here are some points about slides that you need to keep in mind:

1. Slides can be used for Clarifications

Clarification is vital in public speaking because if the information you are trying to convey is unclear, listeners might end up getting confused or worse, misled. Slides used as presentation aids can help get the message across clearly; this is especially helpful if you need to make a point that is visual in nature, or if the information is quite complex.

2. Slides Can Be Used to Emphasize a Point

You can use your visual aid to further emphasize you point. For example, you can use charts, diagrams or statistics to give emphasis on your talk about sexual harassment to assist you in saying that it is a serious concern. When people see numbers, they also become aware that what you are presenting is factual, and you have the data to back your thesis statement.

III. Presentation Aids Can Be Used To Help the Audience Recall A Point

Another function that your props or your visual aids can serve is to increase the likelihood that the audience remember your speech.

Here are some points that will show why presentations can help you drive your point.

1. Learning is Visual

Albert Mehrabian, a professor in University of California, Los Angeles researched into how we take in information during a presentation. He concluded that 55% of the information we take in is visual and only 7% is text.

Essentially, being presented with an illustration or an image is better than having bullet points in a presentation. It can serve as a reminder or a memory aid for the audience.

2. People Remember Through Steps

Ever remembered receiving a course outline from your college professor at the start of the semester? Usually, a person could retain information more effectively if it is presented using a step by step approach, compared to when it is presented in a big paragraph or disorganized manner. Help them remember all the information by providing a specific outline that would help them remember your idea through chronological events, or by simply providing them pointers that would help them retain the data in their heads.

3. A Bookmark for Yourself

Using your presentation aids while practicing your written speech will enable you to be more familiar with your speech. In short, it can serve as a bookmark to remind you where you are in your speech. That way, you can ensure that you would never be lost in your thoughts, and should that happen, you can feel your way back to the main idea that you were trying to expound on.

For instance, if your goal is to inform the audience about your experience with stroke like Dr. Jill Taylor, you might plan to put in your presentation slide simple words like, "The Morning Of the Stroke" or "When I Woke Up". Be it an image or just phrases, it would help you remember your train of thoughts to get you back to the talk.

IV. Presentation Aids Spice Up Your Speech

Dr. Jill Bolte Taylor presented an authentic, preserved human brain in front of the audience. That simple presentation aid was a smashing enough, because unless you're a brain researcher like her, you won't likely see a real human brain every day.

Presentation aids make your talk more interesting. It is true that quality content and excellent delivery can already make a good speech, but a good speech can be made great by the appropriate use of presentation aids.

Qualities of a Good Presentation Aid

Visual aids are essential to helping your audience better understand the key points of your presentation. It should not overwhelm people and should also not distract their attention that would eventually cause them to drift off from you. An effective visual aid will include the following attributes:

1. Seen and Heard By Everyone

Your presentation aid must be big enough and viewable by all of the audience members in the room. If you're planning to use a video, the audio must be loud and clear enough for everybody to hear. Do not think about using anything that cannot be clearly seen or heard – that might distract your audience and point their attention to criticizing your presentation aid.

2. Can Be Easily Operated or Held

In addition, you should be skilled in using the presentation equipment. And also, your presentation aids should be able to help you and not distract you while speaking.

3. Pleasing to the Eye

The design of your presentation should not detract from the content of your speech. Keep your presentation simple so people can focus on the content rather than on the animation or colour. Your visual aids should be based on the outline and ultimately the written speech that you have made.

4. Simple and Easy To Understand

If you put in too many words in your slides or presented too much props on stage, then the audience may not be able to understand the takeaway message of the presentation. Tip: Rehearse. A way to test if your visual aids are addressing the key point is to ask someone who is unfamiliar with your presentation if they can understand what the key point is. If they cannot determine the key point, it may be a good idea to revise your visual aids to include less non-essential information.

5. Serves as Mere Support for the Speech

Visual aids are useful to help the audience better understand your topic if they are used as a complement to, and not a substitute for, your presentation. For example, a visual aid that replaces a presentation could be a PowerPoint that includes big blocks of text that the presenter reads word for word. This will most likely bore the audience members who will not gain much from the presentation.

Preparing Your Visual Aids

If you have never made slides or visual aids before, you should assess your own skill level first. You can make great simple slides if you stick to photographic images or you might want to work and consult a designer. Your TEDx event organizer should be able to help you.

Here are some tips that could help you in making your visual aids:

Props should be supportive of the topic of your speech; they should also be visually stimulating Whenever you use the visual aid, make sure that the attention is on you, and not on the prop. The audience would check out your prop but you should steer them to the right direction – refocus them to you. Just like Dr. Jill Bolte Taylor did with the human brain, she asked an assistant to take it off the TEDx stage to focus on her speech.

When you reveal your visual aid, make sure you continue speaking to the audience not to the prop. Handouts can also serve as your visual aids. Some speakers prefer to give handouts at the end of their speech.

Creating a Presentation Slide

Aside from the usual PowerPoint presentation, there are new ways of making presentation slides that are commercially available to the public. Some of them are also downloadable from legitimate sources in the Internet. If you are bored with the common format that PowerPoint has, you might want to consider experimenting with programs like Prezi, Powtoon, Emaze and Focusky among others.

Here are some tips to help you make your presentation slide:

It would be recommended to use images and photos. If you would watch TED-style talks, most of the speakers use images to convey a point.

Try to use graphs or even info graphics to make a complex idea easier to understand.

One idea at a time. One slide, one idea.

Avoid cluttering one point with a lot of text. Most of the time, audience are bound to read them and not listen to you.

It would be wise to check also the technical aspects of the computers that the organizers will be using for the talk.

In PowerPoint or Keynote, make use of broadcast-safe zones. Don't leave any information or visuals in your slide's corners.

Use big font sizes. Forty to fifty font size is recommended.

Choose a common font like Calibri, Helvetica, Cambria or Verdana. Avoid using fonts that are too stylish and difficult to read. If you are thinking using a custom font, make sure to have a copy to be given to your organizers before the event.

Be original. Post you own content. Only use images that have permission to use. If you have to use something that is not yours, at least cite your sources.

The use of a visual aid will not save you from your poorly constructed speech – one will not stand well without the other. Yet, it is important to know that a good speech can be made even better with the strategic use of slides.

Alas, you have all the things you need for your TED-style talk. The last process of preparing for your upcoming speech is for you to rehearse.

Chapter 5: Practice Makes Perfect

"Practice is the one habit that transforms a merely good presentation into a TED-worthy performance" says communications expert Carmine Gallo in his Forbes article regarding the habit that all speakers do before making a TED talk. "And not just a little practice, but many, many hours of it. Rehearsing your presentation begins well before the PowerPoint slides have been built. To "practice," means internalizing the content so well that your delivery sounds less like a formal speech and more like a conversation over dinner."

Most people would moan out of the way just to avoid rehearsals. They assume that the speech is finished once the script has been written or the visual aids has been prepared and thought of. But if you think about it, writing a speech and preparing for a speech are two different things. You are not fully prepared until you have spent time doing what exactly you should be doing on stage: standing on your feet and delivering your message.

Rehearsing is one of the most important yet often neglected methods in preparing for a production number like a TED-style talk. Some people think it is boring or they may feel embarrassed to stand in front of a mirror and rehearse out loud, simply because it seems fake.

Another reason would be is your high confidence in your expertise. Just because this is your field doesn't mean you no longer need to practice. You think that you know the topic so well that you do not need to talk about it. Another one is that you think you'll do better if you don't practice too much, that you'll be more spontaneous and natural.

Tell you what, those are all just excuses.

Carmine Gallo cites musician Amanda Palmer and her delivery of her presentation at TED 2013, The Art of Asking. "Given her experience performing on a stage one would think Palmer would be comfortable giving a short presentation." But one should remember that giving a performance is different than delivering a speech or a TED talk. Palmer is a performer explains why she spent countless hours over four months to get it just right. Even musicians practice long days in getting their right rhythms and their movements onstage.

Before speaking in the event, Dr. Jill Bolte Taylor managed to rehearse her speech for about two hundred times. After it was uploaded online, the video went viral with fifteen million views and eventually Oprah invited her to discuss it in her show, and even got a book published about her topic, Stroke of Insight after they auctioned the publishing rights.

Stroke of Insight became the second most viewed TED talk of all time.

Imagine the hard work of delivering a speech and the sweetness of the fruit of labour that you would reap afterwards.

Try to incorporate these for your rehearsal before the big curtain:

1. Rehearse until it feels comfortable.

Just practice your speech until you feel completely comfortable even when in front of other people. Moreover, rehearse with different sets of people. Talk to your loved ones, people who are not familiar with your field, your enemies, and strangers in a bar, your drinking buddies and others. Listen to their criticisms and their comments. If somebody tells you that you sound "over-rehearsed" or inauthentic, this means that you sound too formal; you do not sound natural so your audience is not likely to find you credible. Just keep rehearsing to master the flow and content but you should eventually try to focus on talking as if you're speaking to only one person spontaneously, albeit in a one-way conversation.

2. Rehearse with your visual aids.

Nancy Duarte mentioned in her blog that she printed and cut out her presentation slides and re-arranged her message and even added sticky notes until she was content with the flow of the speech. You can practice holding your props until it feels comfortable to handle them.

3. Rehearse while timing yourself.

Remember that you are doing a TED-style talk. This is a speech given in a limited time, and you wouldn't want to spend those precious minutes zoning out and rambling just because you didn't practiced your speech beforehand. Nancy Duarte writes in her blog, that the shorter the talk that means it would take longer for you to rehearse it. In her TED talk case, for an 18-minute talk, it took approximately 18 hours to rehearse. Get a timer and set it to 18 minutes. Try to trim down your words in order to fit the time. Record your progress as you go along.

4. Rehearse your body language.

Your posture also says a lot about your talk. Don't fret about getting the words ideal, but do feel the words, as a lively assembly of your body. Ideally, you might want to videotape yourself and review your performance later.

You might want to get over your camera shyness by recording yourself during practices. This will help you into being used to facing your audience and the camera. Also, you can review your performance. Go back and listen to the audio and do some improvisations.

5. Rehearse the flow of emotions.

Remember that a TED-style talk is also a journey. A good speech makes the audience feel the emotions and can even take them into an intellectual journey. Find out how you would be able to shift from one emotion to another as you go along. Most people are too plain, because they are hesitant about showing their emotions while speaking or discussing a point. And that is boring.

6. Rehearse in the main stage.

A good idea is to visit the place where you will be delivering your speech. Think and plan how each visual aid would appear with you. Plan and rehearse your entry and how move as you talk. You can ask your organizer for some time in order to do a dress rehearsal, along with the timer and your presentation aids.

Chapter 6: Own Your Talk

Do you know why TED talks are so popular lately? It is because they are one of the warmest approaches in conveying an idea in the modern times. They are sunny and make a lasting impression to the audience. And delivering one is not only beneficial to you as the speaker Think of it as an opportunity for people to listen to your message. It feels special because you are not there to sell yourself; you are there because you wanted to impart a part of you in other people's mind. Talking about something that you are passionate about is a gift for you as well, and you give that same gift back by allowing your ideas to flow from your mind to another.

As the date of your speech nears, you might want to reflect back on the preparations that you have done.

Think about the main idea that you want to convey. Of course, during the course of making an outline and script for your speech, you had added in details and sub-plots to form your body. Question yourself if it is still congruent to your beliefs and your aim.

Preparing a speech is a journey and the destination is the audience that you would face on that day. The lessons that you learned as you go along every detail of your message will be ingrained with you. And what you get after delivering such message will also impact the next steps that you would do. It would be a good training for you to conduct such talks: it would not only foster confidence, it would also help you meet a lot of people to be able to expand you universe.

They say that it would take months for TED speakers to be fully-prepared for their talks. If you think that you are not a natural speaker, so are they. It would take tremendous expertise to deliver a message effortlessly in such a short time, in such a way that the audience will remember you.

TED talks gained prominence not because of the people who had given the thought. Some people would think that no one would bother to listen to them anyway, so why prepare? Remember that people will not remember you for what you said, but for what you made them feel. And this is one of those talks that you make your audience feel important. You make them feel such importance by unveiling them your great idea. This is your passion, your life meaning, something that you would want to pass on for generations and generations.

Conclusion

Thank you for reading this book!

I hope that you have learned not only how to create a TED Talk style of lecture, but also how to generate great ideas and a personal style on how you can confidently and successfully convey your thoughts to your audience.

Even if you are not scheduled for a TED Talk anytime soon, know that the tips and techniques that are mentioned in this book would be helpful in every lecture or speech that you are going to make, even outside the TED stage. For that reason, the next step that you need to make is to ensure that you make use of the personal style that you have created in your mind while you are reading this book whenever you go out there to talk about the concepts that you have in mind. You can trust that you will always create a better impact with that TED Talk style that you have created through this book.

Lastly, if you enjoyed this book, please do not forget to rate it at Amazon.com and leave your comment as well. I'm looking forward to hearing from you soon!

Additional Resources

The Public Speaking Cheat

http://www.deepthoughtpress.com/speaking-cheat

Overcome your fear of public speaking, the easy way.

Printed in Great Britain
by Amazon.co.uk, Ltd.,
Marston Gate.